The Skunk at Church . . .
Has His Own Pew

Bob Malcomb

Order this book online at www.trafford.com
or email orders@trafford.com

Most Trafford titles are also available at major online book retailers.

Printed in the United States of America.

ISBN: 978-1-4907-5149-8 (sc)
ISBN: 978-1-4907-5148-1 (e)

Trafford rev. 11/19/2014

www.trafford.com
North America & international
toll-free: 1 888 232 4444 (USA & Canada)
fax: 812 355 4082

Contents

JANUARY

new resolutions

Humor in The Bible...

When an angel told Sara she was going to have a baby, she chuckled at the thought of a 90 year old having a baby. Her son was named Isaac which means "Laughter".

Elijah challenged the prophets of Baal to call down fire from heaven; they couldn't. He laughed and suggesting their Gods were sleeping or deaf, or possibly their God was in the bath room. (original Hebrew).

These are examples of humor in the Bible, but it's only a start. The Jews have spent so much time in persecution; they became experts at humor. (Have you noticed how many Comedians are Jewish?) One of their favorite forms of humor is stretching things FAR out of proportion.

Jesus was the greatest teacher who ever lived. Comedy is a powerful teacher. Understanding the Jewish humor of exaggeration sheds new light on some of his messages;

"Why are you worried about the splinter in your brothers' eye, when there's a barn beam sticking out of your own?"

"You strain at a gnat and swallow a camel."

What do Rodney Dangerfield, Pat Pulson and Jonathon Winters have in common? They found a cure to their depression; humor! (Prov 17:22)

Doctors say 90% of people's medical problems comes from how they think. Ulcers, high blood pressure, weight problems, skin rashes, even wrinkles, are a result of worry; not turning problems over to God. The Bible has the prescription...

The 3 Killers		**The Prescription (1 Corr 13)**
1. Bitterness	....	Faith in God's Long Term Plan
2. Depression	....	Hope in a Good Future (Jer29:11)
3. Unresolved Anger	....	Love those that hate you

New Years Resolution: Alternatives to Losing Weight
* ★ Hang out with people heavier than you...
* ★ Dress in black (like a storm cloud rolling in)
* ★ Wear a full length mirror (People will say, did you see a head floating by; now that's thin!
* ★ Mount a mannequin on your shoulder; go as Siamese twins

★ Wear loose fitting clothes (like a circus tent)
★ Accept it. Dress as Santa…

ANTI-STRESS DIET

Breakfast: 1 grapefruit
1 slice whole wheat toast
1 cup skim milk
Lunch: 1 portion lean steamed chicken & spinach
1 cup herbal tea
1 Hershey Kiss
Afternoon: Rest of Bag of Kisses
Dinner: 1 family size pizza
2 halves garlic bread
4 bottles of soda
Bedtime: 1 Sarah Lee Cheesecake (stressed spelled backwards = desserts)

TYPES OF PEOPLE
- **There are three types of people; those that can count & those that can't…**
- **There are only two types of people in the world. The kind that think there are only two types, and ones that don't.**

"***Pleasant Words*** are as a honeycomb, sweet to the soul, and health to the bones." (Prov 16:24)

LAUGHTER: 1. Distracts your attention from the Problem
2. Reduces our Expectations
3. Increases Endomorphs
4. Reduces Tension

ACTUAL NEWSPAPER CLIPPINGS
Free farm kittens, ready to eat.
Nice parachute: Never opened. Used once. Slightly stained.
Georgia peaches. California grown 0.89 $/pound
Nordic Track $300. Hardly used. Call Chubby.
Lawyer says client was not that guilty.
Hummels! Large selection. "If it's in stock, we have it."

Since God has given me a cheerful heart, he will forgive me for serving him cheerfully." (Joseph Hayden)

A young monk was required to take a three year vow of silence in at a Monastery, high up in the mountains. At the end of the first year the Priest said you may say 2 words. He replied "Bed hard."

The monk went back to his chores, his daily Bibles study and prayer and the recopying of scriptures. When his second year was up, the Priest congratulated him and allowed him two more words. He said, "Food-- bad." Then he went back to work.

Finally the great day came when the Priest shook his hand and told him the three years had been completed. "And how was the experience?" he inquired. "Horrible!" the Monk replied...

"Well I'm not surprised", said the Priest, "You've done nothing but complain since you got here."

"A glad heart makes a cheerful countenance... a cheerful heart is a continual feast." (Prov 15:13-15)

MINISTER'S GOOD NEWS – BAD NEWS
Good: You baptized seven people in the river.
   Bad: You lost two of them in the current.
Good: The Women's Class voted to send you a get-well card.
   Bad: The vote passed 31 to 30.
Good: The Women's softball team finally won a game.
   Bad: They beat the men's softball team.
Good: Attendance rose dramatically in the past two weeks.
   Bad: You were on vacation those weeks.
Good: The Deacons want to pay your way to the Holy Lands.
   Bad: They want to wait until the next War.

"It's never too late to have a happy childhood." (Anonymous)

A Methodist Minister met 3 Baptists playing golf. He invited them to their church grand opening. Sure enough, they showed up. The Minister leaned over and told the Usher "Get three chairs for my Baptists friends." The Usher said, "Pardon me?" So the Minister said louder, "Three chairs for the Baptists!" The Usher turned around to the congregation and said, "OK everyone lets give three cheers for the Baptists. Hip hip harrah!"

After the talk, the Youth Pastor asked all the children: "And where do you want to go?" "HEAVEN!" they all shouted.

Then he encouraged "And what do you have to do to get there?"

One little voice said "Die?"

"Just because you are miserable doesn't mean you can't enjoy your life." (Annette Goodheart)

One woman confessed to the Diet Club; "My family ate half of the German Chocolate Cake. I had to look at it as I was cleaning up. First one thin slice, then another. Before long it was all gone!" She sobbed. The other women all felt bad for her. One asked, "What did your family say?" "Oh" she said, "I was too embarrassed to tell them so I baked another one and ate half of it."

"If it weren't for the brief respite we give the world with fool-ishness, we would commit mass suicide like lemmings." (Groucho Marx)

The minister announced next weeks sermon would be on Noah and the Ark. A couple of boys notice something interesting, so after the service they glued some of the pages together. The next Sabbath the minister started reading "Noah took unto himself a wife and she was (turning the page)... 50 Cubits wide and 30 Cubits high..." He scratched his head, "I've been studying this book for 50 years and I still find things I never noticed before."

"Don't worry. Be happy." (Meher Baba)

BUMPER STICKERS
Be Fishers of Men. You catch 'em. He'll clean 'em.
A clean conscience makes a soft pillow.
A family altar can alter the family.
A lot of kneeling keeps you in good standing.
Are you wrinkled with burden? Come in for a faith lift.
Fear knocked. Faith answered. No one was there.
Truth decay? Brush up on your Bible.
He who angers you, controls you.
If you kneel before God you can stand before anyone.
God doesn't call the qualified. He qualifies the called.
If God is your Co-pilot – swap seats.
Kindness is hard to give away—it keeps coming back.
We're too blessed to be depressed!
Wisdom has two parts: 1) Having a lot to say. 2) Not saying it.

"Worry doesn't help tomorrow's troubles but it does ruin today's happiness."

Did you hear about the dyslexic atheist? He laid awake at night wondering if there really was a "Dog".

Did you hear about the dyslexic heavy metal singer? He sold his soul to Santa.

How many Unitarians does it take to screw in a light bulb? …We can never really know.

NEVER make a Unitarian mad. They will burn a questions mark in your yard. Why is there no Unitarian choirs? Because they always reading ahead in the songs to see if they agree with the words.

Ye Ole Church Bulletin Mistypes
Sue Johnson's Solo; "It is Well with my Solo"
After the Sandwich Luncheon, there will be medication
If you heave during the Postlude, do so quietly.
Don't forget the Men's Annual Goof Outing
Please sign the Information Sheep
Fifth Sinday is Lent
For the word of God is quick and powerful, piercing, even to divide the soup and spirit…
Don't forget our shut-ins during bath weather.

"Corr 13: Love Wins"

> Love is patient Love is kind.
> It doesn't envy It's a state of mind
> Love doesn't boast. It isn't proud.
> Love isn't touchy And it isn't loud
> Love keeps no record of others' wrongs
> It's a trusting, hoping never ending song.
> Love's never happy with an evil end.
> It preserves; never fails. In the end, love wins.

"Sometimes I wish I would have been born smart, instead of so durn' good lookin"

FEBRUARY

The month of love

BIBLICAL METHODS FOR FINDING A WIFE
(4) Kill a 9'6" giant and get a princess for a reward (David)

(3) Buy your X-wife back for 10 Bushel of Barley. (Hosea)

(2) If a relative dies, marry the widow. (Boaz, it was the law)

(1) Marry your half-sister. (Abraham)

"Finally found 'MR RIGHT'. But I didn't know his first name was ALWAYS..."

CHRISTIAN PICKUP LINES TO TRY:
(5) Before tonight I never believed in Predestination...

(4) I hear there's going to be a love offering after the service...

(3) I think you may be sitting on my Bible...

(2) My prayers are answered...

(1) Paul said it is better to marry than burn with desire... Well, when
I saw you I was afraid I might spontaneously combust...

Things NOT to say on a Date...
* I used to come here all the time with my old girlfriend
* I never said you NEEDED a nose job. I said one wouldn't hurt.
* I don't like this restaurant but I had a two-for-one coupon.
* Could you excuse me? My cat gets lonely if it doesn't hear my voice on the answering machine.
* I refuse to get cable. That's how they keep tabs on you.
* When are you due?
* I've finally accepted I'll never find a woman smart as me.

"Nothing is more beautiful than cheerfulness in an old face."

Things women asked me
Are you joking or is this really your car?

Do you consider your job... important?

Is your paycheck big enough to ...take me to McDonalds?

"Joy is not in things. It is in us." (Ben Franklin)

**"The search for happiness is one of the chief sources of unhappiness."
(Eric Hoffer)**

Are these compliments?

I like you toupee. It says "I have better things to spend money on"
"For as much as you eat, you're really not that big."
"I see by your clothes, you aren't materialistic."

I must have brought home an entire sorority of gals for mom to meet, one at a time. She didn't like any of them. I finally found a gal that talked like Mom, walked like Mom, she even thought like Mom. Mom loved her. Dad didn't...

Fake Feeling Good... If you learn to fake cheerfulness you will actually start feeling happier." (Jean Bach)

"I can run the United States, or I can keep up with my daughter Alice, but I can't do both at the same time..." Teddy Roosevelt

"I'm not a vegetarian because I love animals. I'm a vegetarian because I HATE plants!"

My Dad could drink more whiskey, smoke more cigarettes, out cuss, out shout, out spit anyone. And he had the ugliest dog too. He was my anti-example.

I go to a hippy dentist. He lays me back in the chair, turns the gas on, then puts the mask on HIMSELF.

Sign at Church: "Baptist Women's Auction" – I guess they have women for sale? ...I am planning on going.

BECOMING

There once was a girl who loved everyone.
She could find "good" in every situation.

Sure, she met attitudes, she hoped would go away,
But to mention them aloud, would surely make them stay.

So she winked at their faults and continued to look for beauty
In their underlying motives; how they met their duty.

It seems when she praised others "good" (though sometimes small)
It squeezed out the "bad" till it wasn't there at all.

She'd share her good impressions. They'd say "Yeah, guess I am."
Reliving that nice warm feeling; they'd do it over again.

Her friends all loved her dear; felt happy when she was near.
She didn't love them for what they'd done, but for what they... could become.

What was God thinking when he invented Marriage???

WHAT does a boy, who's spent all his life with other boys, living in a house of brothers, KNOW about living with a woman? NOTHING!

If he has to submit a resume to his future father-in-law, it would be a blank sheet of paper. "Well sir, I like the way they look, that's about all I know…"

If it's gross, guys like it. If it's big, guys love it. If it is loud, that's even better and if you can take it apart, or better yet—blow it up, well, it doesn't get any better than that… These are NOT useful skills for marriage.

When I was in high school, I ran into a gal I liked. My mouth got dry. My mind was spinning. Luckily my brother had already coached me not to say something like "gee you're pretty" He said "Give them a compliment, but be specific."

I said "That's a great scar on your forehead!" The poor girl shrieked and ran.

"A guy that says his wife is not the boss of the house, would lie about other things too."

Congressmen should start wearing NASCAR outfits… so we will know who is sponsoring them…

My brother. Paul's great. When I need advise, I just tell him my problem. Whatever he tells me to do, I do the OPPOSITE and it turns out right…

DESPITE THE POPPY SEED ON YOUR TOOTH, AND UNTWEEZED NOSE HAIR, I CAN LOOK YOU IN THE EYES AND TELL YOU I LOVE YOU UNCONDITIONALLY…

"If you wear a rubber nose for a week, your life will be changed because you will get in touch with the joy you can bring to the world." *(Patch Adams)*

When I was a kid, every time I told my family I wanted to be a comedian, they laughed...

THE RECESSION HAS BEEN SO HARD...

I got a pre-declined credit card... CEO's are now playing miniature golf. Exxon-Mobil had to lay off 25 Congressmen. I saw a Mormon with only ONE wife. If the bank returns your check marked "Insufficient Funds," you ask if they meant you or them. McDonald's is now selling the 1/4 ouncer. Angelina Jolie adopted a child from America .Parents in Beverly Hills fired their nannies and had to learn their own kids names. My cousin had an exorcism but couldn't afford to pay for it, so they re-possessed him !Some Americans were caught sneaking into Mexico. Pictures are now only worth 200 words.And, finally.... I was so depressed, I called the Suicide Hotline. It was some lady in Pakistan. I told her I was suicidal, so she asked me to drive a truck load of dynamite.

I feel so honored to have been able to be on the space shuttle, twice. I remember as we took off; thinking how proud my family must be. But I had the oddest feeling in space, not weightlessness, but how spongy the floor of the space craft was. Then it occurred to me it was all a dream. I was standing up in bed.

"Why are you taking so long to hit the golf ball ?"

"My wife is up there by the clubhouse watching..."

"Well you can't hit her from here

MARCH

windy stories for a windy month

The waitress stopped the man, "I am sorry sir but you must have a tie to get in here." The man looked thru his car trunk. All he could find was his jumper cables, so he swung them around his neck. The waitress stopped him and stared, then finally said, "Well, ok you can go in. Just don't START anything!"

Just as the florist delivery van was getting ready to pull out, the manager came running out saying there was a cancellation. Looking at all the flowers in the back the helper asked "which one"... He said "The one that reads 'I will love you forever"

Gary loved the Lord. He had a good job but you'd never know it by the rusted out yellow Vega he drove. But he drove it in pride, like a badge of honor. Because he knew in his heart all the money he was saving by driving an old wreck, allowed him to support missionaries; college friends who were now serving the Lord overseas...

There was nothing Gary loved to do more than witness about God. But Gary had one weakness; golf...

One Saturday morning he showed up at a course he'd never played before. He spied a tall fellow with a full crop of black curly hair, preparing to tee off. Gary heartily introduced himself. The man's name was Jim. As Gary had hoped, Jim invited him along.

As they made their way to the second hole they passed by the parking lot. Jim spied the little yellow Vega covered with big brown rust spots. He pointed it out to Gary and gave a hearty laugh. Jim chuckled "What kind of a guy would drive a car like that?"

But Gary's mind was on other things; ways he could talk about God; How little importance things of this world are." He didn't know what to do when Jim made fun of his car. Come to think of it, it WAS pathetic, so Gary laughed too...

You may not recognize that as a white lie, but it was. A chuckle said "I agree with you. That sure is a sad excuse for a car. I don't know who owns it..." He didn't actually say it but it was implied... Little did Gary know what a HUGE mistake... For the next question out of big Jim's mouth was "What car do you drive?"

Oh-oh... What was Gary to do? Embarrass Jim? Loose his oppor- tunity to witness? He stammered "Ah... that black one over there." Hoping it wasn't Jim's car and they'd move on to another subject.

Jim approvingly said, "That black Monte Carlo looks nice. But they're big. What kind of gas mileage do you get?"

Gary: "Ah... 24 MPG I think..."

Jim: "24, on a Monte Carlo? That great! I've never heard of such a thing. Who works on you car?"

Gary: "Oh it's a... a little place on the edge of town. you probably haven't heard of it."

Jim: "Oh, try me. I probably have. I'm a car salesman it's my business. I LOVE cars. I try to learn everything I can."

Gary was starting to feel sick inside. After all these lies, how could he witness about Jesus Christ? How could he tell Jim, God had taken away his sinful nature? Luckily it was only 9 holes and not 18... But the questions kept coming...

"Where did you buy the Monte Carlo?
"Did you buy it brand new?"
"Did you get a good deal on it?"
"Did it have the same problems as other Monte Carlo's?"
"Have you taken the Monte Carlo on a long trips?"

Gary's head was reeling from all the lies... He started thinking things like "Maybe God would be merciful and just strike me with a lightning bolt right there, and put me out of my misery...

Finally they finished but what was he going to do? He had to wait for Jim to leave so he wouldn't be seen getting in his Vega...

The longer he hung around, the longer Jim talked... he excused himself and tried to hid out in the bathroom... It seemed like a good plan, but...

Suddenly Jim burst through the door; "Gary, Gary are you in here?" You won't believe it. Some guy just got in your Monte Carlo and drove away! Right in broad daylight! Don't worry Gary we're going to call the police and fill out a report. I'm going to stay RIGHT HERE with you thru the whole thing..."

A man from up in the hills didn't help his wife with gardening, kids or even hold down a job. He just sat in the rocking chair on the front porch. In fact he was so lazy he didn't even rock. It bothered men in the neighborhood so they decided to give him a little scare and ordered a casket from the local carpenter.

When they arrived at his house, one of them said, "Elmer you're no good for no one. We've decided to just take ya out and bury ya." He didn't say a word. So they loaded him up in the casket and headed for the grave yard. He didn't object; just laid there.

One of the men started feeling guilty and said, I've got some corn at my house. Why don't we give him one last meal?" Suddenly Elmer raised up and said, "Is it shucked?" "No" they replied. Elmer laid back down, "Go on then."

(Linda Malcomb)

A minister's wife went to the doctor. When he examined her he found pieces of celery in her ear and a piece of carrot in her nose. "What's wrong with me Doc?" She said. "Simple, "He said, "You're not eating right."

I took a date to a Festival. She said "You like festivals, arts and crafts and you even like talking. You are as much fun to hang out with as a gay guy!"

A carrot and a celery stick were close friends. They went every where together. They discussed their feeling about their girlfriends to each other and questioned the very meaning of life. They walked and talked ALL night.

Suddenly the carrot was hit by a car. The ambulance came, his friend jumped in and said prayers all the way to the hospital. He sat nervously for four hours outside the surgery room. Finally the doctor came out with a sad look on her face... She looked him in the eye and said, "I have good news and bad news." He stammered, "Well tell me the good news Doc!" "Your friend is going to live." She said, "...but he will be a VEGETABLE for the rest of his life!"

The Mighty Hunter

I come from a long line of hunters. My father and his father before him. My brothers. They have amazing stories. Even my brother's 9 year old nephew got a deer. Me? Nada! I decided to get serious. I got up at 3:00 am like all good deer hunters do. I bought a devise so I could climb a tree. You can actually sit on the devise after you climb up. For some crazy reason deer never look up. You are supposed to rope yourself in so you don't fall out when you fall back to sleep. Many a fella broke a leg.

I washed my clothes with a special soap that had no smell. Then I sprayed my body with deer urine… Day after day… no deer… I could hear shooting all around me…

My cousin, who was not a hunter, stepped out his back door. There was a buck with a perfect rack, eating corn. He reached inside the door for the gun and plugged it. He made the front cover of Deer Hunter Magazine. They gave him hunting clothes to put on, over his bib overalls, so when he held up the rack for the magazine cover, he'd look like a hunter.

As I was driving to work, a buck ran across the road. That night, I grabbed my gun and headed for the woods where I saw the deer. It had rained that day so I could walk with stealth. Deer like cedar thickets. The pine needles are soft to lay on. In the winter the cedar block out the cold wind. Suddenly I saw the deer lying down. My heart was beating wildly. Was it sportsman like to shoot a resting buck? Frankly I didn't care. I couldn't let a 9 year old kid get ahead of me. I shot him!

Strange! He didn't jump and run. That could only mean one thing. I made a great shot, right thru the heart. As I was shaking, I slowly walked toward the deer. What if he suddenly jumped up and ran straight at me?

Finally I nudged him with my gun. He didn't moved. I couldn't see where I hit him. I decided to gut him and drag him out to the road. But the deer was stiff as a board. I had tracked down and shot… a DEAD deer. His head hangs on my wall to this day.. that's how I became the "Might Hunter".

I was having a family get-together. At the last moment I realized I needed to run to the store. As I was pulling out my brother Howard was pulling in. I told him I'd be right back. He went on in. In a few minutes the phone rang. It was my brother Paul. Since he was calling my house he assumed he was talking to me. Since Howard thought I was calling back to the house to tell him something, he too thought he was talking to me. I don't know the confusing conversation that ensued, but I wish I had a recording of it.

<u>Desperate with thirst</u> a man in the desert waved down a camel driver. "Please sir, may I buy some water from you?" "I don't have any" said the camel driver but check out this nice selection of ties." "Are you crazy?" he stammered as he drug himself on. Suddenly on the other side of the oasis he saw it... a cantina with neon lights and music. He told the door man, "I am so glad you were here, I thought I was going to die of thirst." The doorman replied, "Sorry sir, but you cann't get in here without a tie."

A nearby town is rather poor. Instead of a floor one family used skids from the factory. Each night at the dinner table they had a guest. A ground hog would climb out of his hole, up thru the skids and take his usual place at the table. But they were a Christian family, the ground hog had been trained to put his paws together as they said the dinner prayer. (Gary Perkinson)

My brother Howard is a barber. People are always telling him tall tales. But when they tell a story about something SO dumb they did... well why would anyone make that up? Examples:

"I'm afraid of heights so when I had to get on our roof I tied a rope to myself. I was looking for something to tie the other end to, that would be heavy enough. The car bumper looked pretty good... And you guessed it, I was halfway done fixing the roof when my wife came running out of the house and jumped into the car. I resisted at first but she just gunned the gas and rocks were spinning so up over the house I came and down the other side, and I landed in the grass. Luckily she saw me and I didn't get dragged to town."

"A deer walked so close, under my deer stand I decided to rope it with the extra rope I had with me. I used the rope to hold my self to the tree. I did a good job of catching it around the neck and it bolted away at full speed. That's when I realized the rope was tied to me, and not the tree. I came flying out of the tree and was dragged half way across the field before I got my pocket knife out and cut myself free."

Every time I tell the guys at work I am going to be a comedian, they tell me not to quit my day job...

*Nitrate Definition; **Cheaper than the Day Rate***

*Varicose Definition: **Close By***

<u>Quotes by Lincoln</u>:

"If I were really two faced, would I be wearing this one?"

"I am a success today because a friend believed in me and I did not have the heart to let him down."

"I don't like that man. I need to know him better."

"The question is not 'Is God on our side' but rather 'Are we on HIS side."

I am not saying my daughter talked early but I'll never forget the day she was born… She looked at me like she was trying to form words. Suddenly she said, "Are you my dad? Did you buy me an outfit? Is it pink? On and on she went for the next …18 years.

<u>ROMANS 7: MAN'S STRUGGLE</u>

God is spiritual. I am carnal.
I don't know why I do what I do.
The "good" that I "should" I often don't.
The "evil" I must stop, Sometimes I won't.
But I don't do it, It's the sin IN me.
I look at myself; Nothing good I see.
I delight in God But inside my mind
A fight goes on most all of the time.
Wreck that I am, Please rescue me;
A prisoner of evil who longs to be free.
Thanks be to God Through Jesus Christ;
Forgiveness greater, Than my deceiving life.

So Elmer how did you like the big city ?

I went to a football game. They flipped at quarter then for the next two hours they was runnin and wreslin' and everyone was hollerin "Get the quarterback !"

"Be kind to Nurses. They are the ones that keep the Dr from accidently killing you."

I asked a little girl why she was bare foot. She looked at me funny and said, "These are baby feet ! Bears have hairy feet !"

APRIL FOOLS

"If any man among you seems to be wise in this world, let him become a fool, that he may be wise." (1Cor 3:18)

"April 1 is the day we are reminded of what we are the other 364." (Mark Twain)

"A man who lives free of folly is not so wise as he thinks."

Clowns...
"A clown is like an aspirin, only it works twice as fast." (Groucho Marx)
"It is meat and drink to me to see a clown." (Shakespeare)
"A good clown caricatures his fellow men; a great one parodies himself." (Pierre Mariel)

"He who is aware of his folly is wise. (Yiddish Proverb)

Clones are People **two**
If a **Cow** laughed, will milk come out her nose?
Bumper Sticker: Think "**Honk**" if you're telepathic.
Nostalgia isn't what it used to be.
I just put in **skylights.** Boy are the people upstairs mad.
If you can't be kind, at least be **Vague.**
Honk if you love peace and quiet.

As the college student delivered the pizza, the man growled, "What's the usual tip?" The student said, "The others students said I'd be lucky to get a quarter out of you." Is that so? "grunted the man, and he gave him a 20 dollar bill. "By the way" asked the old man, "What is your major?" The student said, "Psychology"

"If every fool wore a crown, we should all be kings." (Welsh Proverb)

Ben sliced his golf ball deep into a ravine. He grabbed his 8-iron and climbed down the bank. Suddenly he spotted something shiny. On closer examination it was another 8-iron, attached to the hand of a skeleton. Ben screamed to his golfing partner, "Jerry I've got big trouble down here!" When Jerry came to the edge he said, "It's worse than I thought, throw me a 7-iron."

"I was not born a fool. It took work to get this way." Danny Kaye

A young couple borrowed their neighbor's yard ornament, a large goose, and took it on vacation. They had a polaroid camera. So they took a picture of the goose looking at various sites around the USA. Each time they would immediately mail the photo to their neighbor. Within a few days they got their first picture in the mail. Their goose in front of Mount Rushmore. It went on like this for 2 weeks; their goose in front of Ole Faithful, their goose at the Rockies. They returned and was able to keep it a secret for 6 months until one night when their neighbors visited and told them the story. They laughed so hard, they gave themselves away.

Real friends are those that watch you make a fool of yourself and do not feel it was permanently done." *(Anonymous)*

DIFFERENCES BETWEEN WOMEN & MEN

<u>Men</u>: The restaurant check comes to 22.50 Each of the four men throws in a 10 dollar bill.
<u>Women</u>: Gets out her calculator.

<u>Men</u>: have a razor, shaving cream and shampoo in their bathroom.
<u>Women</u>: have 400 items, most of which are unidentifiable to men.

<u>Women</u>: love cats.
<u>Men</u>: say they love cats, to women, then kick them when the women aren't looking…

<u>Women</u>: call eachother names like Sue, Mary Ellen…
<u>Men</u>: call eachother names like Loser and Meathead…

<u>Women</u>: do laundry every couple days.
<u>Men</u>: wait until they are totally out of clothes & have to wear a trench coat to the laundry mat.

MORE CHURCH BULLETIN BLOOPERS

>The church will host an evening of fine dining, superb entertainment and gracious hostility.
>Place your donation in the envelope, along with the deceased person you want to remember.
>The ladies of the church have cast off clothing of every kind. They may be seen in the basement on Friday afternoons.
>Potluck dinner at Sunday 5:00 pm. Prayer and medication to follow.
>This Morning's message: "Jesus Walks on Water" Tonight's message: "Searching for Jesus"
>Low Self Esteem Support Group will meet Thursdays at 7 PM. Please use back door.
>Weight Watchers meeting at the Baptist Church at 6 PM. Enter thru large double door on the east side.
>Ladies, don't forget the annual rummage sale. You can get rid of those things not worth keeping around the house. Bring husbands.
>Remember in prayer those who are sick of our community.
>Counseling available at the church office. Don't let worry kill you. Let the church help.

>In the minutes, Susan bates sang "I Will Not Pass this Way Again" giving obvious pleasure to the members.

>This Wednesday there will Christmas caroling. Bring a blanket and come prepared to sin.

>This Saturday will be the annual pancake breakfast. We need as many electric girdles as possible.

>Bean supper Thursday evening in the basement. Music will follow.

>A church auction will be held on Saturday night. Proceeds will be used to cripple children.

"We must all learn *to live together as brothers, or we will all perish together as fools." (Martin Luther King, Jr)*

A new prisoner kept hearing people call out number, then everyone would laugh. He asked what was going on. Another prisoner explained they only knew so many jokes, and they had all heard them so many times they simply numbered them to save time.

"Oh, "He said, "Can I try? Nine… (no one laughed) … seventeen… (no one laughed) … one… (still no one laughed).

Another prisoner patted him on the back and said, "That's all right. Some people can tell a joke and some can't…"

"If I want to look at a fool, I only have to look in the mirror." (Seneca)

CONCRETE GEESES

I gotta' get a concrete goose
But I'm not quite sure of it's use.
They must be good for somethin'
Cause my friends all got one;
I just gotta get a concrete goose!

Why, I'll bet it has a many a use!
A Valet for my clothes,
Bustin' up ice that's froze,
To rest my foot to shine my shoes,
I got ta' get a concrete goose.

Cleanin' muddy boots with it's tale,
Use it to hammer a really big nail.

A target for the paper boy,
For the weight lifter–a bath tub toy.
Everyone can use a concrete goose.

To make kids happy when they're feelin mean
They can turn the goose over on Halloween.
Dress it up as Santa or Uncle Sam
Or a Turkey, or Bunny, or a Lepri-CAN
I'd be so festive with a concrete goose.

Why, I could use it to attract other gooses.
They'd waddle in my yard all day,
In the bird bath and play,
I gotta' get one right away,
Cause it has so many uses.

Interviewer: **How did you get 900 women to marry you?**
Solomon: **No no, 300 wives.**
Interviewer: **Oh yes, that's right. And 600 concubines.**
Solomon: **That's right. I was practically a bachelor.**
And that's a common misconception. The original scripture said combines.

ACTUAL TEST ANSWERS

Test: What is Hard Water ?
Student: ICE

Test: Name 6 Artic Animals
Student: 2 polar bears and 4 seals

Test: Name the wife of President Roosevelt
Student: Mrs Roosevelt

Test: What is puberty ?
Student: When a boy enters Adultery

Test: Where is Hadrian's Wall ?
Student: Around her garden

MAY

ADOPT-A-PET MONTH

"Lord, Help me to be the kind of
person my dog thinks I am.."

Baptist Dog

A Pet Store advertised a "Baptist dog" so a lady wanted to see it. The manager called out fetch. Sure enough the dog came back with a Bible. He said "Palms 23", sure enough, the dog knew how to drop the Bible open to just the right page, so they took him home.

They wanted to show their friends his tricks so they had them over for dinner. The couple was impressed but inquired if he could do any regular tricks. So the couple tried "HEEL"…

Instantly the dog put on paw on the guest, bowed his head and started to doggy-pray. That when they realized they had been deceived! They had purchased a PENTICOSTAL dog!

CATS

- *There is no snooze button on a cat that wants breakfast.*
- *In the cat's eyes, all things belong to him.*
- *One cat just leads to another.*
- *Dogs have owners. Cat have staff.*
- *Call a dog; he'll come. Call a cat; "they'll get back to you".*
- *Pharaohs worshiped cats as Gods. The cats never forgot.*
- *Cats KNOW how you feel. They just don't CARE.*

"Happiness is a warm puppy." (Charles Schulz)

A fella explained to a Pastor his dog had been feelin poorly. He thought if he had him baptised and prayed over, maybe that would help. The pastor explained there was a Catholic church just down the street that might do it. The fella asked, "How much would something like that cost? I only have $5000." The Pastor said "Well why didn't you say your dog was a Baptist?"

FREE KITTENS! *Everywhere I go I see that sign along the road. What's the deal? Is there a country where kittens oppressed?*

*About dark I got in my car. It had been a nice day. My arm was out the window. I looked into my rear view mirror. There sat **SATAN** in the back seat! I turned away. I GULPED. I could hardly believe it. When I got up nerve I looked again. Yep it was him. His horns were black and his eyes glowed! I stopped the car and slowly turned around. A black kitten was sitting on my headrest… "meow".*

THINGS I LEARNED AS A CHILD

(1) No matter how hard you try, you can't baptize a cat…

(2) You can't trust a dog to watch your food…

(3) If your Mom is mad, don't let her brush your hair…

*"**Happiness is like a cat***. *If you try to coax it or call it, it will avoid you. It will never come. But if you pay no attention to it and go about your business, you'll find it rubbing against your legs and jump into you lap." (William Bennett)*

One Saturday dad walked up behind Mom and said "Would you like to go out girl?" Mom turned around and gave him a big hug and said she'd love to. At the end of a wonderful evening he finally confessed he had been talking to the dog, lying near Mom's feet.

*<u>**A man followed a woman**</u> out of a movie theater. He said, "Excuse me. I couldn't help but notice your dog really enjoyed the movie; he cried at the sad parts, and laughed at the funny parts. That is really unusual." "Yes" the woman said thoughtfully, "that is strange, because he hated the book."*

<u>DOGS</u>
> My dog is worried about the economy. Alpo is up to $3 can. That is 21 in doggy dollars.
> If you say silly things to a dog, he will look at you and as if to say "Wow, you're right. I never thought of that." Dave Berry
> The average dog is a nicer person than the average person.
> If your dog is fat, YOU aren't getting enough exercise.
> My dog has many friends! He wags his tail instead of his tongue.
> There's no psychiatrist in the world like a puppy licking your face.
> Dogs may be the only thing on earth that loves you more than they love themselves.

*A **Pet Store Parrot** squawked "You're Ugly You're Ugly!" to a female customer. She tried to ignore him as she walked around the store but every time she got near, he insulted her again. The manager saw it, apologized profusely, took the parrot in the back room where there was much shouting and squawking. He returned the parrot to it's perch, where it sat quietly with it's head drooped.*

The lady made her purchase and started walking out. As she passed the parrot, they locked eyes. The parrot looked left, then right and said "…You know!"

Two guys out for a stroll with their Doberman & Chihuahua. The first guy decided to go in and get something to drink, so he says "Do what I do"… He puts on his sunglasses, walks over to the doorman and says "This is my seeing eye dog." The doorman says "Wait a minute. A Doberman?" The man says, "Yes, they are using them now. They are very good."

The doorman lets him in, then the second fella' walks up. "This is my seeing eye dog." The Waiter says, "Sorry sir but you're going to have to do a lot of fast talking to get me to believe a Chihuahua is a seeing eye dog." So the second man says, "What? A Chihuahua? They told me it was a German Shepherd."

TAPE TO YOUR BATH MIRROR:
1. There are at least 2 people in this world who would die for you.
2. At least a dozen people in this world love you in some way.
3. The reason someone might hate you is they want to be like you.
4. A smile from you can bring happiness to anyone (even if they don't like you).
5. You mean the world to someone.
6. Every time you make a mistake, something good comes out of it
7. Remember the compliments. Forget the rude remarks.
8. Every night, someone thinks about you before they go to sleep.

3 men, stranded on an island, found a genie-bottle She told them she'd give them each a wish. The first asked to be back with his family "Poof!" The second asked to be with his Bible Study group "Poof!" The third guy looked sad. "I really miss my friends." "Poof" They were back !

I want to die in my sleep, like my Dad... not screaming my head off, like his 5 passengers...

Women think they are so superior because the left and right hemispheres of their brains have 23% more nerve interconnect-ivity than a man's brain... They can answer the phone, bake a meat loaf, iron a shirt and watch a baby, all at the same time.... I can too... I held the meatloaf, baked the baby and answered the iron... I went to the doctor. He asked "But how'd you burn the other ear ?" I said, "They called back."

I saw a sign of a wooden stork in the neighbor's yard. I told my 80 year old Dad, "Oh they must have a new baby..."

He said "How do you know ?"

"There is a stork in the yard."

He said "Oh dear, I forgot to have that talk with you.."

A 90 year old couple went out on a blind date. The woman came home upset. Her daughter asked her why.
"I had to slap his face 3 times" she said.
"He got fresh ?"
"No, I thought he was dead."

JUNE
THE MONTH OF WEDDINGS

For their wedding, a young couple asked their minister to read 1st John 4:18 "There is no fear in love, but perfect love casts out all fear." But the program left out the "1st" so John 4:18 was read instead; "It is true what you say, you are not married but you have been married and the man you are now with is not your husband."

A husband and wife were seeing a marriage counselor because he wasn't being romantic enough. The counselor asked the husband if he knew his wife's favorite kind of flower. He proudly exclaimed he knew that one "It's self-rising, isn't it honey?"

MARRIAGE

* *Women have more of an imagination that men. They have to, so they can tell us how wonderful we are...*
* *Married men should forget their mistakes. No use two people remembering the same things...*
* *There are two times when a man will never understand a woman... before marriage and afterward...*
* *Married men live longer than single men, but married men are more willing to die...*
* *Only two things are necessary to keep a woman happy (1) Let her think she's having her way, and the other is... to let her have it.*
* *Can you imagine a world without husbands? No crime. No Wars. And lots of happy fat women..*

"A happy marriage is a long conversation which always seems too short." (Andre Maurois)

After the service the Minister planned to call the couple down front for their marriage vows, but for the life of him, he could not remember their names. "Will those wanting to be married please step forward? he requested. Nine single ladies, two widows, and five teens stepped forward immediately.

"When someone does something good, applaud! It will make two people happy. (Samuel Goldwyn)

At their 60th Wedding Anniversary a couple was ask their secret for success. The wife said, "Before we married I promised my husband he could all the major decisions and I'd make all the minor ones." The husband added, "So far it has all been minor decisions."

After an elderly woman died, she left specific instructions for her memorial service. "NO male pallbearers!" Said she, "They wouldn't take me out when I was living, so they aren't taking me out after I'm dead!"

As a funeral procession slowly drove by, a golfer stopped in mid swing, took off his hat and bowed his head. When his golfing partner commented on how impressed he was with his reverence, he replied, "Well, after all, she and I WERE married for 40 years."

A couple up in the hills often got on each others nerves. But the husband broke the cardinal rule of never disagreeing with your spouse in front of company. In the middle of her mouse story he kept correcting "It was a rat". Finally she gave him that look that he knew all too well, and he made for the back door. But she was right behind and caught him at the well. There was a scuffle and down he went into the watering trough again and again. As she was holding him under the water she suddenly came to her senses and pulled him out. When stopped sputtering and coughing he exclaimed, "It was a rat." *(So now when a family member realizes we are being stubborn, we put humor back into the conversation by saying "It was a rat!")*

Things Husbands wish Wives Knew...
1. If you think you're fat, you are. Don't ask me. I refuse to answer.
2. Sometimes we are not thinking about you. Live with it.
3. Don't ask what we are thinking about unless you are prepared to discuss power tools, monster trucks or Civil War Battles.
4. When we have to go somewhere, ANYTHING is fine to wear.
5. Come to us with a problem if you want us to solve it. That is what we are. Men solve problems. Women give sympathy.
6. Subtle hits do not work. Strong hints do not work. Obvious hints do NOT work. Just say it!
7. If something we said can be interpreted two ways; and one of the ways makes you sad or angry. We meant it the other way.
8. If you want us to act like the soap opera men, dress like the Victoria Secrets women.
9. Christopher Columbus didn't need directions and neither do I.

LADY BUMPER STICKERS
SO MANY MEN - SO FEW WHO CAN AFFORD ME.
GOD MADE US SISTERS - PROZAC MADE US FRIENDS.
COFFEE, CHOCOLATE, MEN SOME THINGS ARE JUST BETTER RICH.
DON'T TREAT ME ANY DIFFERENT THAN YOU WOULD THE QUEEN.

I used to be a cosmonaut. They sent me on a rocket to Venus. Everyone there is just like us, except they are upside down. They have wheels on their hats.

I could not get the hang of the hat. I kept falling "up". I had to walk around using my feet. They thought I was very strange. They asked me if it hurt to use my feet. I said, "No, everyone on earth does it."

They said, "We have 2 hands and 2 feet to work with, but you only have two hands. It must take a long time to do your work?"

I said, "Yes, we work 8 hours a day, then usually go home and work another 8 hours."

They said, "Wow! We only work 1 hour a day."

"I told them I had an uncle like that, and he wouldn't work that long if Aunt Ethel didn't hide the remote."

They said, "Your uncle was probably from Venus.

I said, "I always suspected it was something like that."

Everyone on Venus was happy. They go around smiling all the time. I'm a happy person too. So I went around smiling. But since I was upside down to them --it looked like I was frowning. They asked "What is wrong? What is wrong?" So I had to remember to frown when I was happy and smile when I was sad.

What did I learn from my trip to Venus? That it is very HARD to be sad when you are smiling.

"Until I Met Sheila" (I think it's a country song)

I was just a country boy; with holes in my bluejean knees.
Until …I met her… Oh how she has changed me!

She threw away my clothes, just 'cause they had tears and stains,
Spent a whole day tryin' outfits, I'll never go to a Mall, again!

Now I dress like a sissy, when I go to church;
Lookin' all rich and prissy. Even have to tuck in my shirt.

She's traded in my canoe, for a motorized pontoon
And set a flower arrangement, in Grandpa's brass spittoon.

Her mangy dogs, she says "Is part of MY family now"
But every time she looks away, the big one sneers and growls,

She traded my ole pickup, for a shiny Cadillac.
She says "Don't muck it up!" …I want my pickup back!

She says "Wash your dishes every Single Day..
And wash the rest of you too, if you're wantin' ta' stay!

I usta' love meat and taters, veggies turn my toes!
Nowdays salads and 'maters, are comin out my nose.

She says theres' things in MY frig that's got a life of their own.
I know just how they feel, I remember when I had… One.

I was footloose and free, could do anything I want…
And really, really lonely… come to think of it.

Of snakes and snails, and puppy dog tails…
I've had enough! But this bein' civilized, is still sorta tough.

IT Support: "I need you to right-click on the Open Desktop."
Customer: "Ok."
Support: "Did you get a pop-up menu?"
Customer: "No."
Support: "Ok. Right click again. Do you see a pop-up menu?"
Customer: "No."
Support: "Can you tell me what you have done up until this point?"
Customer: "Sure, you told me to write 'click' so I wrote down click."

I put an ad in the paper "Wife Wanted". Two days later I got a 100 letters… all from men.
They said "Take mine"…

A prisoner in jail receives a letter: "Dear Husband, I have decided to plant a garden. When is
the best time to plant ?" The prisoner replied: "Dear Wife, do not dig up the back yard. That's
where I hid the money." A week later, he received another letter: "Dear Husband, Men came
with shovels and dug up the yard." The prisoner wrote: "Dear wife, now is the best time to
plant."

My brother took his mother-in-law for lazer cataract surgery. She hadn't been able to see for a
long time. The next day they took off the bandages and she looked in the mirror for the first
time in 20 years and said "That lazer was so hot it wrinkled up my skin.

JULY
MISSIONS MONTH

*"**The best way** to cheer yourself up is to cheer someone else up." (Mark Twain)*

Visiting other countries is FUN, but even in countries where they speak English it can be confusing. For example in ENGLAND...

Cookie	....	Biscuit
Biscuit	....	Cookie
Torch	....	Flashlight
Bonnet	....	Car Hood
Lorie Tipper	....	Dump Truck
Takeaway	....	Take out
Roller Booting is	....	Roller Scating
Hill Walking is	....	Hiking

RUSSIA... if you pull out in front of someone... (they will shake their fist and say "You smell like a billy goat!"
> *... if you send 12 roses she'll cry all night. An even number of flowers means death.*
> *... "Spice-Cee-Ba" means thank you and*
> *... "Yellow Blue Bus" means "I love you"*

AFRICA... people may not be able to read, so the photo on the label is what is inside... Gerber Baby food doesn't sell very well.

CHINA... "Our Chicken is finger lickin good" was translated into... "It's so good, you will eat your finger." "Pepsi brings you back to life" translates... "Pepsi brings your ancestors back"

SAUDI..."Jolly Green Giant" became... "Big Green Ogre"

MEXICO...The car "Nova" sales were way down. Suddenly they realized they needed to change the name... "No-Va" means "It won't go"

When I was a kid I had a drug problem. Every Wednesday and Sunday I was DRUG to church.

"Happiness is found in doing, not merely possessing" Napoleon Hill

"We act as though comfort and luxury is the chief requirement for life when all we really need to be happy is something to be enthusiastic about." (Charles Kingsley)

An American was in Japan but he hated the food. To his delight he found a pizza place that delivered. Thirty minutes later he takes the pizza from the delivery boy and starts sneezing. He says, "My goodness, what is wrong with me? What is on this pizza?

Delivery boy bows deeply and says, "We put on it what you order, pepper only."

One of the things I keep learning is that the secret of being happy is doing things for other people." (Dick Gregory)

It's so nice of China to translate signs into English for tourists…
    Slip Carefully
    Shicken Resturant
    Deformed Man Lavatory (handicapped?)
    Because you are dangerous – no enter!
    Touch wire instant death $200 fine
    Police Tip: avoid being stolen
    Do not jump in elevator. If you do it gonna be stop. And you must
    be locked up!

"If you want others to be happy, practice compassion. If you want to be happy yourself, practice compassion." (Dalai Lama)

If the world could be represented by 100 People…
- 70 would be Non–Christian, 30 Christian
- 52 would be Female, 48 Male
- 57 Asians, 21 Euros, 8 Africans, 6 Americans
- 6 own 60% of the world's wealth
- 1 would own a computer, 1 would have a college education
- 70 unable to read, 50 would suffer malnutrition

Things to THANK GOD for…
- 1 million will die this week, did you wake up healthy?
- If you attend church without fear, you are ahead of 3 billion.
- If you have food and clothes and bed, you're in the top 25%.
- If you have spare money in a dish, you're in the top 8%.

Complaints to the Rexburg Idaho Police Department

- neighbor wearing skimpy bikini
- mean squirrel
- children not minding
- angry note left on trash barrel
- lost TV remote
- neighbor's shrub trespassing

Walking thru a Grocery Store

"Vow, Milk Powder? Look! Powdered Eggs? Und give a look here! Vats dis? Baby Powder? America, vat a country!

I'm bicycling thru Germany. I ask Vern "How do you say GOOD DAY to a young lady..."
He says, "That's simple... "Ick Lieben Zee mine Shots-ee."
But all the fraulines kept saying... I DON'T THINK SO.
Finally I ask one gal how do you give a German greeting. She says "Guten Tog means "Good Day" and Wie Gehts means "How goes it?"
I asked well what have I been saying... She said "Ick" is "I"... Lieben is "love"... Zee means "you" so... Ick Lieben Zee Mine Shotzee means "I love you my darling..." NEVER trust a guy named "Vern"

That's when I decided maybe I should learn a little of the language of the country I was in. I knew "thanks" was "Danka" I saw a book called "Positiv Dinkin" which was about Positive Thinking" of course. I thought, hey this is pretty easy. Just replace the "TH" with a "D" Sure enough I went in a McDonalds —all the waste baskets it said "Dank U"

HOLLAND

Bicycling in Holland was great, lots of flat land... the women were a head taller than me...

I was camping out in a field. I set up my tent beside my bike, got in and laid down. I could hear Gospel Music coming from some kind of community building. So I decided I better check it out. Everyone is praying and testifying and singing with their hand up... then I saw it.. they had a CASH BAR in the back of the room. Everyone was offering to buy me a drink. They were really "in the SPIRIT"

I ask them about Christmas... They said "you Americans with your North Pole, reindeer and Elves" — that's SO silly...

Everyone knows Saint Nicholas is from Spain... he arrives on a boat with his 6 white horses pulling a sled... Oh yes and he has 8 black helpers. It used to be 8 black slaves but now everyone tells their kids, no no, they're just his FRIENDS...

Bad kids in the USA used to get coal for Christmas when they were bad... compared to Holland, that's pretty mild. Bad kids there used to get a kick, or worse, Saint Nicholas would kidnap them and take them back to Spain...

They have a big festival with music and Saint Nicholas arriving in his boat... The parents are laughing and happy, until they look at their little traumatized Dutch kids;... they don't know whether to be excited... or run and hide...

ENGLAND

If a Lori Tipper hits your auto and it's leaking petrol, you better get a torch out of your boot. Translation: a dump truck, a flash light and the trunk.

Two boys who lived with their Grandma. They were about to go to bed. The older son prayed about the day he had and about everything he had done. The younger son he prayed much louder. He prayed for bikes and toys. When he finished the older brother asked him "Why are you praying so loud? God is not deaf" The young boy said "Yeah, but Grandma is."

First Ole Man: I ache all over !
Second Ole Man: I feel like a new born baby... No teeth,
no hair and I think I just wet me pants...

Knock Knock
Whos' there ?
Dishes...
Dishes who
Dis is da police. Come out with your hands up !

AUGUST
COUNTRY FOLK

YOU KNOW IT'S A SMALL TOWN WHEN....

...the "Welcome To" sign is on the back of the "Now Leaving" sign

...Garbage Trucks are in the annual Parade.

...the PTO Bake Sale makes front page news.

...they have a First Street but not a Second

...everyone in town has one of three last names

...anyone from out of town is considered a "Foreigner"

...Volunteer Fire Dept refers to a barn fire 5 years ago as "Big One"

...Crisis Phone Line is the same number as Edna's Beauty Salon.

Elmer came into his Lawyers office and says, "My wife says she wants a DEE-vorce. What should I do?" The Lawyer asks "Does she have any grounds?" Eb says, "Yep, she got over 100 Acres." "No no!" the Lawyer corrects, "Does she have a case?" Eb relied, "No, no Case tractor, but we got a good John Deere." The lawyer says, "No! WHY... WHY does your wife want a divorce?" Eb says, "She claims we have trouble communicatin'."

Country Dating Tips:

1. Always bait your girlfriends hook, especially on the first date.
2. Clean dirt behind fingernails as it detracts from a gals rings.
3. Give compliments like "Your eyes are the color of Windex."
4. Even dogs with good table manners should not be invited.
5. A clean bowling shirt will give a sporty appearance.
6. With enough aftershave you don't need to bathe.

"I can live 2 months on one good compliment." Mark Twain

Why all this interest in the "Sock Market" being up or down?

Elmer went to the big city and got robbed. All the thief could find was a quarter. He said, "You really put up a fight for only twenty five cents!" Elmer said, "I thought you were after the $500 in my shoe."

(**Andy Griffith** tells this one) A fella was "breaking in his new apprentice to be as smart as him". He told him to run in the hardware store and get some 4 x 2's... Otis went in a asked but the Sales Clerk said, "We don't have any 4 x 2's. Are you sure you don't mean 2 x 4's?" Otis said "I'll go check." ...A couple minutes later he came back all out of breath "Yeah, we need 2 x 4's." The sales clerk said "How many do ya need?" Otis said "I'll go check." He came back and said "100". So the sales clerk asked "How long do you need them?" Otis said "I don't know. I'll go check." Again he returned all out of breath and said "We need 'em a LOOOONG time. We're goin'a build a house out of 'em."

A salesman was startled as he rounded the curve and saw a three legged chicken running along side his car. Suddenly it turned into a farm full of three legged chickens. The sales got out and exclaimed "This is the most incredible thing I ever saw!" The farmer in the yard said, "Yep, Ma and the boy, we all three like chicken legs so I bred some so everybody would be happy." "That's amazing" Said the Salesman, "How do they taste?" "Don't know, Said the Farmer, "Can't catch 'em."

(Queer used to mean unusual) Everyone is queer except for me and thee, and thee is a little queer. (That's what the Old Quaker said, and what my mother told me, every time I talked about someone.)

Decorating Tips:
1. Table centerpiece should not contain items from a taxidermist.
2. If you have to vacuum the bed, it's time to change the sheets.

Famous Last Words
… I wonder what this button does…
… I'll hold it, you light it!
… Hey, watch this!
… That's odd…
… Nice doggy!

The little boy seemed to accept his old dog's death without any confusion. We sat together for a while, wondering aloud why animal's lives are shorter than humans. Then he suddenly said "I know why."

"People are born so that they can learn how to live a good life -- like loving everybody all the time and being nice. 'Well, dogs already know that, so they don't have to stay as long…"

'OLD' IS WHEN…. Your friends compliment you on your alligator shoes, but your feet are bare..

Little Boy: Dear Lord, make me be a gooder boy-- but if you can't, it's OK. I am having a good time.

(true story) **A little boy was walking down the aisle in church. Everyone at the wedding was in tears of laughter as they watched him "step – step – then he'd hold his hand up and growl". We he got to the front, the bride asked what he was doing. He said, "I am the ring bear".**

Elmer was given a chain saw and told they expected him to cut down 50 trees a day. But at the end of the first day he only had 25. The head lumberjack told he to try harder. Sure enough by the end of the day he had cut down 30 trees. The supervisor said "Everyone else is cutting down 60 trees a day. is your chainsaw working ok?" and he gave it a pull "Brrrrrr Brrrrrrrr" Elmer said, "Hey! What's that noise?"

You KNOW it's a small town when you see people locking their car doors at the grocery store-- because they are worried someone will fill their back seats with tomatoes.

A gal was at a Christian Singles Retreat and she was seeking God's guidance as to whether she should approach a certain man or not, so she turned to her Bible and let it fall open. The verse was about Zackius. It read "But Lord, after three days he stinkith."

St. Peter says, "Here's how it works. You need 100 points to make it into heaven. You tell me all the good things you've done-- I give you points for each item, depending on how good it was. When you reach 100, you get in."

"Okay" the man says, "I attended church every Sunday"

"That's good, says St. Peter, "that's worth two points"

"Two points?" he says. "I gave 10% of all my earnings to church."

"Well, let's see," answers Peter, "that's worth another 2 points.

Did you do anything else?"

"Two points? Golly. How about this: I started a soup kitchen in my city and worked in a shelter for homeless veterans."

"Fantastic, that's certainly worth a point," he says.

"hmmm...," the man says, "I was married to the same woman for 50 years and never cheated, not even in my heart."

"That's wonderful," says St. Peter, "that's worth three points!"

"THREE POINTS!!" the man cries, "At this rate the only way I get into heaven is by the grace of God!"

"SWING TALE"

Let me tell ya 'bout a gal with really long legs--
But it's normal for a cow; To look that way!
With big brown eyes; That flirt and bat,
And a mouth full o'hay; Let me tell ya where it's at.
When the radio's on; Her tail starts to swing.
Her rear end wobbles; And makes me want to sing.
My hands on her milker; We squirt in-time
I get the beat and start to rhyme.
And all the barn animals join right in...
With a BIG BASE GRUNT; Comin' from the pig pen.
The roosters on the rafter; Starts to crow
As we listen to the songs on the Radio.

Bored at Walmart ?

1. Make a name tag and act official. Tell people if they
   let you ride IN the cart, they get 50% off.
2. Challenge people to duels with stryfoam tubes.
3. Set up a tent. Tell others they are only allowed in if
   they bring their pillow and sleeping bag.
4. Try to put a bag on M&Ms on layaway.
5. Set up a battlefield with G. I. Joe's vs. X-Men.
6. Set up a "Valet Parking" sign out front of the store.
7. Hide in the clothing rack. Say "pick me! pick me!"

Dad,$chool i$ great, making lot$ of friend$ and $tudying hard. I $imply can`t think of anything I need. Ju$t $end a card, a$ I want to hear from you.Son,I kNOw astroNOmy, ecoNOmics, and oceaNOgraphy keep you busy. Pursuing kNOwledge is a NOble task.

SEPTEMBER CHILDREN

Before they entered the temple...

Mary and Joseph looked for Jesus for 3 days with no success. Standing in the busy streets of Jerusalem Joseph may have put his arm around Mary and prayed, "Dear Lord, You gave us the greatest gift mankind has ever know. You trusted us with your only son. Well, ah, we lost him...

Teacher: What commandment tells us how to treat our brothers and sisters?
Student: "Thou Shall Not Kill?"
Teacher: And why should we be quiet in church?
Student: "Because people are sleeping?"
Teacher: Why did Joseph & Mary take Jesus to Bethlehem?
Student: "Because they couldn't find a babysitter?"

A 9 Year Old's Thanksgiving Blessing: *Dear God, We thank thee for the turkey and the rolls and the sweet potatoes and the red jiggle stuff and the bread stuffing, even though I don't like it. We ask that you let us not choke on the food. Amen"*

Ira: I am Jewish. Today for Show and Tell I want to show a minorah...
Mary: I am catholic. Today I am going to tell you about the Crufix...
Stevie: I am a Baptist. This is a casserole...

MOMMY: What did you learn in Sunday School today?
GIRL: A guy named Noah fell out of his beat, but it was OK since an other boat came along and picked him up.
MOMMY: Is that what the teacher said?
GIRL: If I told you what they really said, you wouldn't believe it."

Surpreme happiness in life is knowing we are loved. (Victor Hugo)

What's the difference between a Sadiusee and a Pharisee? A Sadiusee believes when you die, there is no heaven. And that is why he is "Sad You See"...

What do you call a deer with no eyes? No I'dear?
Little girl: "Mommy, why are some of your hairs white?"
Mother: "Well every time you make Mommy cry or disobey me, one of my brown hairs turns white."
Little girl: "Really? ...how come ALL of Grandma's hair is white?"

New Study Reveals: Half of all students below average

After trying for hours to get her daughter to clean her room, the mother exploded, "Get this room cleaned up NOW or I am going to have a cow!" The 3 year old looked quite puzzled and said, "You mean you are going to trade me for a cow?"

Composition by a 6 Year Old
The World is made up of men and women, also boys and girls. Boys are little men. Boys are an awful bother. They want everything they see... but soap. Boys are no good at all, until they grow up and get married. My Mom is a woman and my Dad is a man. A woman is a growed up girl. My Dad is such a nice man, I think when he was a little boy he must have been a girl.

The doctor gave a little boy a vaccination, and put a bandage on his arm. "I think you better put the bandage on the other arm." The boy suggested. "Why?" the doctor asked, "This way your friends will know not to touch it."

The boy said "I don't think you know about my friends."

"Never fear spoiling children by making them too happy. Happiness is the atmosphere in which affection grows.

(Ann Eliza Bray)

The First Grade teacher called a mother, "I am afraid your little girl is going to need a Speech Therapist. She has trouble saying "th".

Mother: "... I vonder vat de mater could be?"

A little boy turning in a purse he found at the mall. The lady that lost it rushed up and thanked him. She looking in the purse and sure enough, the twenty dollars was still there. "That's funny, She said, "When I lost it –it had a 20 dollar bill. Now it has 20 Ones. "That is funny" the little boy exclaimed, "The last time I found a purse for a lady, she didn't have any change for a reward."

Boy: "Mommy, why are you rubbing cold cream all over your face?
Mother: "To make myself beautiful." (a few minutes later the mother took the cream off)
Boy: "It didn't work did it?"

A woman with a baby in her cart at the store was watching the little boy in front of her. He was crying and throwing a temper tantrum. Then she heard the boy's mother say, "No you may not have a baby sister today. That lady got the last one."

The boy hated the outhouse. One day when the creek was swollen he pushed it in and it floated away. That night the boy's father ask if he was the one that did it. The little boy confessed, then his Dad ask him to get his belt and go to the woodshed.

"But when George Washington admitted he chopped down the cherry tree, he didn't get a spanking" the boy protested. Father replied, "Yes but HIS father was not sitting in the tree at the time."

When a female teacher *got her ears pierces, the 3rd grade students were quite fascinated: "Does the hole go all the way thru? Did it hurt? Did they do it with a needle?" "No" the teacher answered, "They used a gun." (silence) Then one child asked, "How far away did they stand?"*

Teacher: *Who can name the four seasons?*
Student: *Sugar, salt, pepper and vinegar.*
Teacher: *Name a disease associated with cigarettes?*
Student: *Death*
Teacher: *What is a fibula?*
Student: *A small lie.*
Teacher: *What is a seizure?*
Student: *A Roman Leader.*
Teacher: *What is "benign" mean?*
Student: *It is what you be, after you be 8.*
Teacher: *What is a Hindu?*
Student: *Lays eggs.*

A little boy was attending his first wedding. After the service, his cousin asked him, "How many women can a man marry?" "Sixteen," the boy responded. His cousin was amazed that he had an answer so quickly. "How do you know that?" "Easy," the little boy said. "All you have to do is add it up, like the pastor said, 4 better, 4 worse, 4 richer, 4 poorer."

After a church service on Sunday morning, a young boy an-nounced, "Mom, I've decided to become a minister when I grow up." "That's okay with us, but what made you decide that?" "Well," said the little boy, "I have to go to church on Sunday anyway, and I figure it will be more fun to stand up and yell."

A 6-year-old was overheard reciting the Lord's Prayer at a church service, "And forgive us our trash passes, as we forgive those who pass trash against us."

A boy was watching his father, a pastor, write a sermon. "How do you know what to say?" he asked. "Why, God tells me." "Then why do you keep crossing things out?"

<u>**Ms. Terri**</u> *asked her class to draw pictures of their favorite Bible stories. She was puzzled by Kyle's picture, which showed four people on an airplane, so she asked him which story it was meant to represent. "The Flight to Egypt," was his reply. Pointing at each figure, Ms. Terri said, "That must be Mary, Joseph, and Baby Jesus. But who's the fourth person?" "Oh, that's Pontius - the pilot!"*

The Sunday School Teacher asks, "Now, Johnny, tell me frankly do you say prayers before eating?" "No sir," little Johnny replies, I don't have to. My mom is a good cook."

A little girl was sitting on her grandfather's lap as he read her a bedtime story. From time to time, she would take her eyes off the book and reach up to touch his wrinkled cheek. She was alternately stroking her own cheek, then his again. Finally she spoke up, "Grandpa, did God make you?" "Yes, sweetheart," he answered, "God made me a long time ago." "Oh," she paused, "Grandpa, did God make me?" "Yes, indeed, honey," he said, "God made you just a little while ago." Feeling their respective faces again, she observed, "God's getting better at it, ain't he?"

☺ **How do you catch a "UNIQUE RABBIT"?**
ANSWER--YOU -- NIQUE up on it!
☺ **How do you catch a "TAME RABBIT"?**
ANSWER--TAME WAY!
☺ **How do you "TOP' A CAR?**
ANSWER--TEP ON THE WAKE! NOW DO YOU FEEL ---TUPID?

<u>**A snail**</u> took a ride on a turtles back. Do you know what he said? "Weeeeeeeeeeee!"

<u>Things Kids Wonder...</u>

➤ Why do people splash toilet water on themselves?
➤ Why would anyone want apple-pie-out'a the comode?
➤ Who invented potato's all-rotten?
➤ How they get the deer to cross at those yellow signs?
➤ If there's no God, Who pops up the next kleenex?
➤ How does a thermos know to keep something hot or cold?

One father was so proud of not limiting his daughter to gender-based toys. He asked her what game she was playing with the trucks and cars. "Well the big truck is the daddy. The big car is the Mommy and the little car is their baby…"

(True Story) One teacher was so flustered with her students having spring fever she threatened the next one that speaks is going to get his mouth taped shut. Rodney couldn't resist. She had him stand up and humiliated him in front of the other students. Years later he was killed in the military. His classmates were in the funeral home recalling funny things about Rodney. Their old teacher was there too. She said "Do you remember the time I tapes his mouth shut?" and she started to cry. "How I wish I could hear him speak one more time."

One of the girls hugged her and asked, "Do you remember what you did next?" You had us all take out a piece of paper and write everyone's name on it. Beside their name you said to write one thing you like about them. The next morning you came in with a piece of paper for each student. On the paper you had a list of all the good things everyone said about them." The young woman opened her purse to show she still kept her list. Her teacher was amazed. She said "I don't remember that at all."

Then several other students produced their list from their wallets and purses… There must be someone YOU love. Make a list and send it to them today, while you still can…

This minister just had all of his remaining teeth pulled and new dentures were being made. The first Sunday, he only preached 10 minutes. The second Sunday, he only preached 20 minutes. But, on the third Sunday, he preached 1 hour. When asked about this, he said "The first Sunday, my gums were too sore. The second Sunday my dentures hurt too much. But the third Sunday, I grabbed my wife's dentures by mistake and couldn't stop talking."

First Ole Man: I ache all over !

Second Ole Man: I feel like a new born baby… No teeth, no hair and I think I just wet me pants…

Woman: "My fiancée is telling everyone he's going to marry the most beautiful woman in the world…"

Her friend: "What a shame, after this time you invested.."

OCTOBER work

A co-worker asked what it was like to be a Christian. "It's like being a pumpkin… You're all alone out in a field when God picks you up. Takes you home, washes you up. Takes off the top, takes the yucky stuff out. Gives you a new look and puts a glow inside you…"

Husband-Zombie Test
1. Is their main function walking and eating?
2. Do they sit and stare at the TV (or other objects)?
3. Do they seldom listen to you?
4. Do they seldom respond?
5. Do they seldom have an original thought or idea?
   If "yes" your spouse might be a Zombie!

"The best way for a person to have happy thoughts is to count his blessings and not his cash." (Anonymous)

Signs you don't have enough to do at Work
1. **You have read the entire joke calendar for the year**
2. **You see Elvis in the shadows of your cubicle wall.**
3. **People come to your office to get pencils—from the ceiling**
4. **You've figure out a way to get off Gilligan's Island.**
5. **You've scanned & Photoshopped a Xerox copy of your face.**
6. **The 4th Div of Paperclips have overrun the Pushpins Army.**
7. **General White-Out extinguished his rubber band artillery.**

Trying to put a little variety into their day, one gas meter reader challenged the other one to a foot race back to the truck. Suddenly out of all the nearby houses, all the other people came running too.

Actual Post-Interview Notes on Job Applicants
- Applicant stretched out on floor to fill out form.
- She wore a walkman and said she had no trouble hearing me.
- Bald candidate excused himself, and returned with a hairpiece.
- She asked to see MY resume to see if I was qualified to Interview.
- Applicant said 'would show his loyalty by getting our logo tattooed.
- When asked about hobbies, he tap danced around the office.
- Interviewee phoned his therapist to ask questions.

"Apologetics means never having to say you're sorry for being a Christian."

Albert Einstein was so tired of giving lectures on a circuit, and his Driver was so tired of hearing them, they decided to switch one night, with Albert driving and the Chauffeur giving the Lecture. The men looked a great deal alike, and no one noticed. After the lecture he even fielded a number of questions brilliantly, but one Professor, wanting to show how much he knew, asked an extremely complex question. Without missing a beat, he said "Why the answer to that is so simple, I'll have my Driver explain it."

A new business received flowers on their first day they were open. They said "Rest in Peace" --But it wasn't half as bad as the wreath at the cemetery that said "Congratulations on Your New Location!"

THE WRONG SIGN
Cleaning Service: **"Able to do the worst possible jobs"**
Florida Billboard: **"If you can't read, we can help"**
California Freeway: **"Fine for Littering"**
Michigan Restaurant: **"Half baked Chickens"**
Bookstore: **"Featuring Rare and Nonexistent Books"**

Auto mechanic reads order "Car makes clunking sound when going around corners" When finished, he wrote: "Removed the bowling ball from the trunk, $20"
The psychiatrist called the father in and told him he had determined the reason his son was always sleepy. "Your son is afraid there is some one under his bed." Explained the psychiatrist. The father asked what he should do. The psychiatrist said, "Well I have dealt with this kind of thing before. If you bring him in once a week for 6 months, your son would be free of fear." The father asked how much would it cost. "Well it's 100 dollars a visit."
Sometime later the psychiatrist ran into the son. He asked him "How are you doing?"
"Great" said the boy "My dad cured me."
"Really" asked the doctor, "And how did he do that?"
The boy said, "He cut off the bed's legs."

A judge with the wisdom of Solomon presided over a case where an number of women in an apartment building were accusing each other of causing problems. He stamped his gavel for order and said, "All right, all right, the oldest woman may speak first..." The case was dismissed.

Jack always thinned down his paint, to make more money for his Contract Painting Company. One day he was high in the air, leaning out on a scaffold painting the Baptist Church. Suddenly the sky grew dark and a bold of thunder struck the ground, knocking him down. As he lay there the rain washed off all the useless paint.

He looked up to heaven and said, "Oh God, forgive me. What shall I do?" Suddenly from a dark cloud a deep voice commanded, "Repaint! Repaint and thin NO more!"

Advise is Cheap

1. The journey of a 1000 miles starts with a broken fan belt.
2. Experience is something you don't get until AFTER you need it.
3. Everyone seems normal until you get to know them.
4. If at first you don't succeed, don't try sky diving.
5. There are two theories on how to argue with a woman. Neither one works.

A minister, late for the **graveside service**, saw the backhoe filling in the hole and a couple leaving. He went over, read a scripture and said a short prayer, then left. The backhoe driver looked over at his assistant, and said "Well I'll be, that's the first time I ever saw a dedication of a septic tank."

Letters from Little Children...

Dear God, I bet its hard for you to love everyone in the whole world.
There is only 4 in our family and I can never do it.   Billy

God, I went to a wedding and they kissed right in church. Is that OK ?

Dear God, Instead of letting people die, why don't you just keep the ones you got ? Kelly

Dear God, In Bible times did they really talk fancy like that ? Jill

Dear God, I am American. What are you ?   Sammy

Dear God, If you look down Sunday, you can see my new shoes. Pam

Dear God, Maybe Cain and Able would not fight so much if they had
their own rooms. It worked for me and my brother.   Billy

Dear God, Did Thomas Edison invent light or you ? I
bet he stole your idea didn't he ? Susie

Dear God, If the dinosaurs were not extinct we would not
have a country. You did the right thing.   Tim

Dear God, Send Dennis Kent to a different camp next year, OK ? Willy

Dear God, Thank you for my baby brother but I wanted a PUPPY.

NOVEMBER ELDERLY

Walking 20 minutes a day adds to your life. This enables you, at 85 years old, to spend an additional 5 months in a nursing home.

My grandpa started walking five miles a day when he was 60..

Now he's 97 years old and we don't know where he is.

I like long walks, especially when they are taken by people who annoy me. I walk early in the morning, before my brain figures out what I'm doing..

I joined a health club last year, spent about 400 bucks.

Haven't lost a pound… Apparently you have to GO THERE.

The advantage of exercising every day is so when you die, they'll say, 'Well he looks good, doesn't he?'

If you are a cross-country skier, start with a small country.

They were going around the table saying things they were thankful for when it came 6 year old Alex's turn. She said "I'm thankful for me!" They ask her to explain… "Well, if it weren't for me, you all wouldn't be as happy." (Alex Sparks)

"Fake Feeling Good… Believe it or not, you actually start feeling happier." (Jean Bach)

A new widow told the minister her husband's favorite song was Jingle Bells and asked if they could sing it at the grave side service. The next day the preacher led everyone in this happy song as slowly and solemnly as possible. When he was done the widow burst, "No it was 'When they Ring those Golden Bells'.

"Do not fear. Fear leads to the dark side" Star Wars

A man goes to Florida. Upon arriving he e-mails his wife to let her know he made it… Only problem is—he misses the last name by one letter and ends up e-mailing a lady who just lost her husband…
E-Mail: "Honey, just arrived. It sure is hot down here. Looking forward to you joining me tomorrow…"

"He who laughs, lasts." (Mary Pettibone Poole)

A lady called the newspaper company to complain she had not received her Sunday newspaper.
"Ma'am today is Saturday"
"Oh" she said ".. that would explain why there was no one in church."

"I've spent a lot of time reading the Bible... looking for loopholes" W C Fields

First Old Man: *:It sure is windy today.*
2ⁿᵈ Old Man: No! It's Thursday!
3ʳᵈ Old Man: Me too! Lets go inside and get a drink.

Grandma said "That was sweet of you to bringing me a cup of coffee, Honey" Then she noticed a little green plastic man in it. She exclaimed, "Oh dear, what's this?" Her grandson said, "You know Grandma, the best part of waking up is soldiers in your cup."

My sister, Linda, was working as a HMO telemarketer. She called and asked to speak to the man of the house. She could hear the elderly ladies feet clip-clopping down the hall.. then stop. Then she heard the feet clip-clop louder and louder and the woman picked up the phone and said, "Oh I forgot. He died 2 years ago."

Signs You Might Need to Increase Your Hygiene:
> Minister puts clothes pin on nose before shaking hands.
> The janitor follows you around with a vacuum sweeper.
> You're the only person sitting on your side of the church.
> When people extend their hand, a bar of soap is in it.
> Special Communion plate, just for you.
> You left a ring in the baptismal pool.

A man was driving his wife and mother-in-law to the beauty shop. His wife said *"You're driving too fast!"*
His mother-in-law says, "No you're not, we're late!"
His wife said, "It's too hot in here."
His mother-in-law says, "No it's too cold!"
This went on for miles with the husband saying nothing...
Finally he pulled over to the side of the road and asked his wife, "Ok, who's driving here, you or your Mother?"

Good decisions come from experience. Experience comes from bad decisions.

"When one door closes, another opens. But if we stand, longing for the closed door, we will never see the new opportunity." Helen Keller

<u>Aunt Ruthie</u>

Where are you, sitting in the den?
The cafeteria, talking to a friend?
Then your eyes meet mine, you sit up and grin.
Hi Aunt Ruthie, its good to see ya!

You get the nurses laughing,
You love to be a clown.
You tell then I'm your boyfriend
And ask me to sit down.

Lets go for a ride, you say,
"I'll take you in to town!"
Hey, who's here to cheer "who" up anyway?
Oh Aunt Ruthie, how I miss ya'.

In the big wheeled chair,
Down the hall we fly.
"Faster, faster" you smile
As the rooms go wizzing by.
Whew... Aunt Ruthie, lets sit for awhile.

I should just see an ole' woman
Who can't think a thought of her own,
But I can't, I see an Aunt
Talking for hours on the phone.
...Oh Aunt Ruthie, so long alone.
...Here we go again, you say "Lets go fast!"
Shouting "I love you" to everyone we pass.
Years of bottled affection, now free at last.
...I wish I could tell you, just what you've been
From little shirts in the mail, to college money you'd send.
For you to die, I thought better, than to end up this way.
But you're happy, full of love, you brighten my day.
"Do you love me honey?" you say, and lean forward.
Yes I do, thoughts of you,
Are in my heart, forever stored.

DECEMBER GIFTS

Grandmother *wrote out $200 checks for each of her family and wrote on the cards "Merry Christmas, buy your own present". After Christmas, she found all the checks neatly stacked in her desk drawer... She had failed to include them in the card.*

If it would have been "Three Wise Women"...

- They would have asked for directions.
- They would have arrived on time.
- They would have had help delivering the baby.
- They would have brought a casserole.
- They would have given practical gifts.

Instruction on Holiday Eating

1. **If you go to a party and they have carrot sticks, they know nothing about holiday spirit. Leave immediately. Go next door where they are serving egg nog and fudge**
2. **Always ask if the mashed potatos are made from whole milk. If not, pass. It's substituting bologna for steak.**
3. **If someone brings gravy, pour it on EVERYTHING. Make a volcano with the mashed potatoes and fill it.**
4. **If you find apple pie, mincemeat or pumpkin pie you. Like make sure to take 3 slices, that's the magical number. Position yourself near what you like best and do not move. Make other go around you.**
5. **Do not snack before going to the party to control your appetite. That's the point. Eat someone else's cooking.**
6. **Life should NOT be a journey to the grave with the intention of arriving safely in an attractive and well preserved body. Rather to skid in sideways, chocolate in one hand, body thoroughly used up, worn out and screaming "WOO HOO what a ride!"**

Xmas in Sweden

The Norse God of thunder is pulled by 2 goats. They do all the usual Christmas traditions. In addition they may put a straw goat on the tree or under it. They also erect a 43 foot tall straw goat in Stock- holm square. It usually gets set on fire.

Ireland Xmas

Stuff a goose with potatoes and put holly and berries on the tree.

Greece Xmas

They start off by eating "Christ Bread' the beautiful centerpiece on the table. Carolers go from house to house and store to store. They get coins for their efforts.

Jewish Xmas

For 8 nights in December, Hebrews light one of the 8 candles on the Menorah. It is a celebration from 165 BC, when Judas Macabee threw the Syrian rulers out of their country. To celebrate, they lit lamps, even though they didn't have enough oil. The miracle of the lights was that it kept burning for the 8 days.

Best Xmas Date

The funniest date I EVER had was with a Recreational Therapist. I complained about all the fun wasted on a holiday like Halloween; where we got to play tricks on people. We brainstormed the problem for a few minutes and came up with an idea...

We went grocery shopping. We laid out paper lunch sacks for all our friends and family we planned to "trick". We wrote their name on a sack, wrote all the things we liked about them, complete with graphics, put a big red ribbon loop around the top, filed it with candy and goodies, went to their house hung it on the doorknob, rang the doorbell, ran and hid in the bushes. It was SO funny.

A little boy ran to Santa and climbed up in his lap. He went into great detail about what he wanted. Later that day, in another mall, there was another Santa. The little boy ran to him to give him a hug. Santa asked, "And what would you like for Christmas?" The little boy stepped back "You really ought'a be writing this stuff down."

"Ever body got it wrong. Angels don't wear halos any more. I forgot why but scientist are working on it." Sydney, 9 yrs old

"It's not easy bein' an angel. First you die and go to heaven. Then there's flight training, then you wear angel clothes." Matt, 8

"Angels gotta' wear dresses, that's why they're all girls. Boys wouldn't go for it." Antonio, 9 year old

"What I don't get about angels is why, when someone is in love, they shoot them with arrows." Sarah, 7

"Angels live in cloud houses make by God's son. He's a very good carpenter." Jared, 8 years old

"Angels talk all the way to heaven when they are flying you up. The main thing they talk about is where you went wrong to make you dead." Daniel, 9

My computer has a button. When you hit it, a cup holder comes out. It says "CD". I think think that stands for Cold Drink...

I'm training for a Micro-Mini Marathon. It's 26 FEET long.

A little boy started a letter... Dear Santa... NO! I need to write to someone more powerful. "Dear Lord" If you send me a bike I will be good for 2 weeks... I can't do that... I'll be good for 1 week... No!... (he runs in the church, gets the plastic statue of Mary)... if you ever want to see your mother again... send a bike."

Ebert and Sigmund walked thru the woods all day. Finally Siggy said, "I'm tired. Next pine tree we come to, I'm cutting it down, even if it don't have lights."

Hip Elderly Texting...

Text: ROTFL Rolling on the Floor Laughing
Senior: ROFLCGU and Can't Get Up
Senior FWIW: Forgot where I was
Senior BTW: Bring the wheelchair
Senior IMHO: Is my Hearing Aid on ?
Senior TGIF: Thank God its 4 (early dinner special)

Miss Belch, a missionary from Africa, will be speaking tonight at Calvary Methodist. Come hear Bertha Belch, all the way from Africa.

Those parking on the north side of the church, please remember to park on an angel.

This being Easter Sunday, we will ask Mrs. Jones to come forward and lay an egg on the altar.

Applications are now being accepted for 2 year-old nursery workers.

Please welcome Pastor Don, a caring man, who loves hurting people.

Ushers will eat latecomers.

Funny-man and stand-up comedian, Bob Malcomb compiled the 1% of humor that he thought was absolutely hilarious, into a book titled "Don't Eat This Book - It Tastes Funny". It will not only tickle your funny bone, but make you a legendary speaker, starting each messages with a memorable antidote.

When Bob isn't doing standup, he is using structural engineering to build Christian hospitals and churches around the world.

He's made many cultural mistakes in foreign countries, but it only gives him more comedy material. He also has a series of Christian Science Fiction Stories, Christian Missionary Adventures and a book on inventions that can help people in Third World Counties.

Bob was raised in a Christian home but became disillusioned with God when he was taught evolution in high school. By 25 years old he saw that science did not solve the difficult issues like conflict resolution, hope, love, loyalty, humility... Bob says the important answers in life come from the Bible, not science.

Bob Malcomb, StructuralEngineering@Live.Com
4134 E Quick Creek Road
Deputy, Indiana 47230 812-595-3003